ANIMAL DETECTIVES

BEDBUG-SNIFFING BEAGLES
and Other Scent Hounds

Rosie Albright

PowerKiDS press.

New York

Published in 2012 by The Rosen Publishing Group, Inc.
29 East 21st Street, New York, NY 10010

First Edition

Editor: Joanne Randolph
Book Design: Kate Laczynski

Photo Credits: Cover, pp. 9, 18, 22 Stan Honda/AFP/Getty Images; pp. 4–5 Philipp Guelland/AFP/Getty Images; pp. 6, 24 (airport) Shutterstock.com; p. 10 Karen Kasmauski/Getty Images; p. 13 Brian Kersey/Getty Images; pp. 14–15 Visuals Unlimited, Inc./Alex Wild/Getty Images; pp. 17, 24 (mattresses) Justin Sullivan/Getty Images; p. 21 Fuse/Getty Images; p. 24 (blood) © www.iStockphoto.com/wellglad; p. 24 (couch) © www.iStockphoto.com/Justin Allfree.

Library of Congress Cataloging-in-Publication Data

Albright, Rosie.
  Bedbug-sniffing beagles and other scent hounds / by Rosie Albright. — 1st ed.
      p. cm. — (Animal detectives)
  Includes index.
  ISBN 978-1-4488-6152-1 (library binding) — ISBN 978-1-4488-6264-1 (pbk.) — ISBN 978-1-4488-6265-8 (6-pack)
  1. Beagle (Dog breed)—Juvenile literature. 2. Hounds—Juvenile literature. 3. Bedbugs—Juvenile literature. I. Title.
  SF429.B3A43 2012
  636.753'70886—dc23
                    2011027091

Manufactured in the United States of America

CPSIA Compliance Information: Batch #WW12PK: For Further Information contact Rosen Publishing, New York, New York at 1-800-237-9932

CONTENTS

Beagles have been used as hunting dogs for many years. They mainly hunt rabbits.

Beagles are well-loved family pets, too. President Lyndon B. Johnson had three beagles named Him, Her, and Edgar.

Beagles are part of a group called scent hounds. They have a great sense of smell.

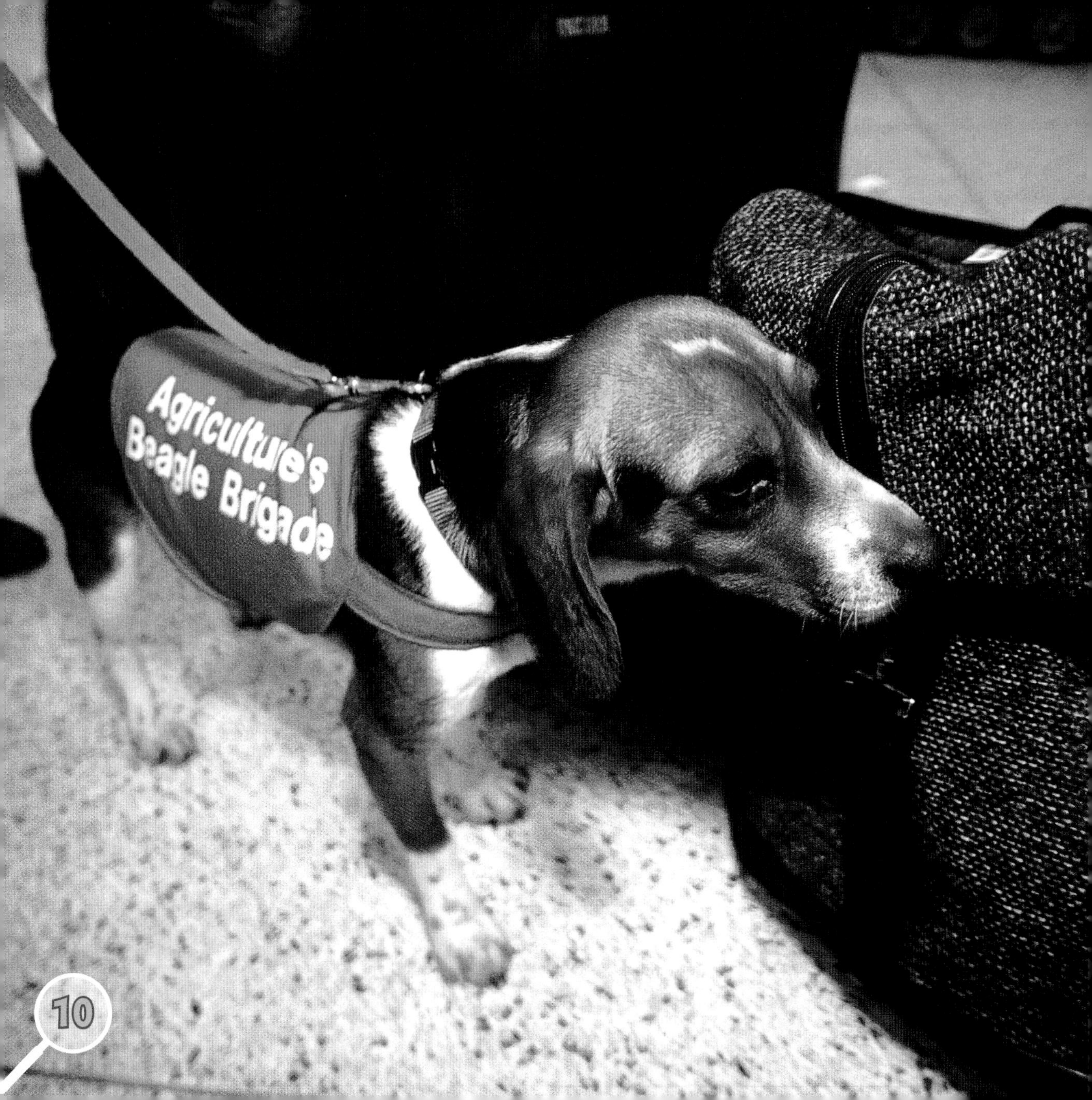
Agriculture's
Beagle Brigade

A government group called the USDA uses beagles. Their Beagle Brigade sniffs out illegal produce at **airports**.

Beagles are trained to find bedbugs. Trainers put bedbugs in cans to teach beagles what they smell like.

14

Bedbugs are small bugs that feed on people's **blood**. They eat at night.

Trained beagles find bedbugs living in **mattresses**. Bedbugs are flat, brown, and wingless.

Beagles can find bedbugs in **couches**. Bedbugs hide in small, dark places.

Bloodhounds and other scent hounds are used to find bedbugs, too.

Beagles and other scent hounds use their noses to help people.

WORDS TO KNOW

airport

blood

couch

mattress

INDEX

WEB SITES

Due to the changing nature of Internet links, PowerKids Press has developed an online list of Web sites related to the subject of this book. This site is updated regularly. Please use this link to access the list:
www.powerkidslinks.com/andt/bedbug/